The Enhanced Reading Resource Reference Book

The Enhanced Reading Resource Reference Book

Dyann G. Sullivan

Library of Congress Control Number:		2011905391
ISBN:	Hardcover	978-1-4628-5174-4
	Softcover	978-1-4628-5173-7
	Ebook	978-1-4568-9318-7

This book was printed in the United States of America.

To order additional copies of this book, contact:
Xlibris Corporation
1-888-795-4274
www.Xlibris.com
Orders@Xlibris.com
97374

DEDICATED TO NATHANIEL HERBERT FOR INSPIRING ME TO BE A
BETTER EDUCATOR, WRITER AND PERSON.

CONTENTS

INTRODUCTION

The Enhanced Reading Resource Reference book was designed to provide a variety of information, to help caregiver, teachers, and parents of young children intensify their reading and comprehension skills; to motivate pre-schoolers and elementary age children to read by making reading a fun and beneficial part of their everyday lives. The reference book will assist the caregivers, teachers and parents to make reading a desirable and creative experience for all participants.

The reference book will give caregivers, teachers and parents a vast supply of tools and resources to enhance and support early language and literacy development for young children. It will also give all participants a great reading foundation, which will stay with them throughout their lifetime.

ACKNOWLEDGEMENTS

I would like to thank my husband, Marvin G. Sullivan, for his loving support in my quest for starting and writing this reading resource reference book. My children, Demond R. Zellner and Shonte` S. Zellner for their love and support in my endeavors. To both my granddaughters, Neshanthia N. Zellner and Jasmine D. Zellner for inspiring me to make "Kelly the Cat" (My stuffed animal, read with me partner). To my mother, Annie M. Gordon, for her loving support, loving memories of my dad, (William A. Gordon), and to all my siblings, (James, Geneva, Patricia, Garrett, Joann, Jerry and loving memories to my baby brother Dennis), for always giving me their encouragement throughout my career as an educator. I would also like to thank my sisters-in-law, (Gwen, Bobbie, Estelle and Pat), nieces, nephews, and closest friends for always being there when I needed someone to talk to. Many, many thanks to my friend Rosa Evans for loving "Kelly the cat", and for always encouraging me to write this book. May God bless each and every one of you.

I would like to especially thank my sister-in-law, Estelle Gordon and my friend Patricia Edge, for assisting me by proof reading and editing the writing in this reference book.

I

READ WITH ME

OVERVIEW

Children should be read to frequently. A suggestion is everyday and/or every night. Reading to them will give children a role model, and a foundation of the importance of reading. Reading together forms a great bond and is an excellent way to prepare and encourage young children to pick up a book and read to themselves. Early experiences, reading books will convey and motivate young children to learn and excel in their development.

SUGGESTED ACTIVITIES

1. The reader will choose a familiar book (Example—"The Three Bears") to read, and then invite the children to join in. Asking and provoking questions while reading the book.

2. The reader will change the sound of his/her voice and encourage the children to change their voices when reading books.

3. The reader will allow the children to pretend to become characters in the book/story.

4. The reader will ask open-ended questions about the book being read, so the children can express their understanding of the book.

5. The reader will allow the children to choose books to model the adult reader.

6. You may be creative and add your own ideals to this list.

_____

_____

_____

_____

_____

SUGGESTED BOOKS

"The Little Red Hen" by Byron Barton

"The Very Hungry Caterpillar" by Eric Carle

"We're Going on a Bear Hunt" by Michael Rosen

"Tell Me a Story, Mama" by Angela Johnson

"No Jumping on The Bed" by Ted Arnold

"Add your own books to this list"

_____

_____

_____

_____

_____

_____

II

READ ALOUD

OVERVIEW

Reading aloud to preschoolers and older children will give them incentives and skills for learning to read on their own. This will encourage them to pick up and read a book without being told.

Reading aloud to children gives them experiences with books, print, and the written words. They will be motivated to want to read and learn new things in their world. Reading aloud is a fun and lively way for families to spend quality time together. Children love to be close to the ones they love.

The caregivers and teachers act as an effective role model, when reading aloud to children. This also extend reading to other activities such as scribbling, drawing, and writing. This can also encourage parents to read aloud to their children.

SUGGESTED ACTIVITIES

1. The reader will read aloud, then encourage non-readers to read with a partner.

2. The reader will read aloud, then involve all participants to take a part in the story.

3. The reader will read a book about food (Example—"Cookies"), then, actually make cookies with the children.

4. The reader will wear a costume, while reading aloud to the children.

5. Add your own interesting ideals to this list.

_____

_____

_____

_____

_____

_____

SUGGESTED BOOKS

"Brown Bear, Brown Bear What Do You See?"
by Bill Martin Jr.

"Chicka Chicka Boom Boom,"
by Bill Martin Jr. & John Archambault

"Bugs" by Nancy W. Parker and Joan R. Wright

"Goldilocks and the Three Bears" By Jim Aylesworth

"Add your own books to this list"

_____

_____

_____

_____

_____

_____

III

WORDLESS BOOKS

OVERVIEW

Wordless books can tell a story about realistic or imaginary characters and their outcomes. They give you a story through no words pictures, or few words. Children can have fun learning to create and tell their own stories by telling what they see in the pictures. Wordless books helps children use their innate abilities to jump start their imagination. Wordless books can excite children to explore new possiblities and creativity. Their exploration will help them to grow and learn new and exciting things.

SUGGESTED ACTIVITIES

1. The reader will allow children to create their own stories in their own words by reciting them to the group.

2. The reader will allow children to help read a wordless book and use rhyme words where possible.

3. The reader will use wordless books to help children build confidence in their ability in reading aloud.

4. The reader will allow the children to read a wordless book and put themselves in the story.

5. Add your own wordless book ideals to this list.

_____

_____

_____

_____

_____

_____

SUGGESTED BOOKS

"Abuela" by Arthur Dorros

"Good Dog" by Alexandra Day

"Changes" by Pat Hutchins

"The Snowy Day" by Ezra Jack Keats

"The Snowman" by Raymond Briggs

"Add Your Own wordless books to this list

_____

_____

_____

_____

_____

_____

IV

READING WITH PROPS

OVERVIEW

A wonderful and fun way to hold the attention of pre-school and school age children is using props. Young children enjoy looking, touching, tasting, and smelling interesting things. The reader is allowing the children to become apart of the story. By using props, this will give young children a hands-on approach to learning and enjoying books. Some props that maybe used are: puppets, toys, objects, animals (real and stuffed), and costumes, just to name a few items.

Props are creative ways to enhance a book/story with young children.

SUGGESTED ACTIVITIES

1. The reader can use hand puppets while reading a book to young children.

2. The reader may hide a stuffed animal in the room or even choose a child to hold the stuffed animal, then reveal the animal at the end of reading the book.

3. The reader may use a handmade worm while reading the book, "The Very Hungry Caterpillar" by Eric Carle, then allow the children to feed the caterpillar by placing play food in the mouth (hold cut-out). You may use a Pringle chip can.

4. The reader will allow children to dress-up and act out the characters in the book/story.

5. Add your own interesting ideals to this list.

_____

_____

_____

_____

_____

_____

SUGGESTED BOOKS

"The Three Little Pigs" by Troll Associates & Illustrated by Eileen Grace

"The Very Hungry Caterpillar" by Eric Carle

"Peanut Butter and Jelly" by Nadine B. Westcott

"What Do You Want To Be" by Lakeshore & Illustrated by Ron Ellsworth

"Add your own books to this list."

_____

_____

_____

_____

_____

_____

V

READING AND MUSIC

OVERVIEW

By combining reading with music, heighten the intensity of children response to reading. Reading and music is an excellent match to encourage children to express the book/story they have read. For example, if the reader played a song called, "The Three Little Pig," by Greg & Steve, then the children are allowed to act out the story by singing the words, and moving to the directions of the words. At the end of the activity, the children would probably say, "let's do it again!" They will remember the book, story, and song for a long time.

They were engaged in the story as well as the music, and had lots of fun learning and moving with their peers.

SUGGESTED ACTIVITIES

1. The reader allows the children to play musical instruments while reading a book to them.

2. The reader and children recite finger plays/poems while listening to music.

3. The children will act out a story while listening to the story set to music.

4. The reader will allow the children to listen to the words of a song; then move to the direction of the song.

5. Add your own interesting ideals to the list.

_____

_____

_____

_____

_____

_____

SUGGESTED BOOKS

"Activity and Game Songs" by Tom Glazer

"Stories and Songs for Children" by Pete Seeger

"Moving to the Beat" by Greg & Steve

"Let's Play Finger Plays" by Tom Glazer

"Play Your Instrument and Make a Pretty Sound"
by Ella Jenkins

"Add your own books to this list"

_____

_____

_____

_____

_____

_____

VI

READING WITH A THEME

OVERVIEW

Themes begins with what children know and see everyday, Caregivers use selected themes to help children enhance their concepts about their community and environment. Using themes will help the caregiver select appropriate books, props, and activities in the lesson plans. Themes can grow from unexpected events that offer rich opportunities for exploration. Encourage children and their families to bring in books, pictures and other materials related to the theme. An appropriate topic for a theme matches the developmental abilities of the children and offers rich opportunities for discovery and exploration. Here are a few examples of themes that could be used: community leaders, farming, occupations, seasons, holidays, and transportation.

SUGGESTED ACTIVITIES

1. The reader will use the theme, "The Community," then bring in a variety of community leaders to read to the children.

2. The reader will select the theme, "Bugs," then allow the children to go out and collect different kinds of bugs.

3. The reader will do a theme on, "Cooking," then plan to cook pancakes with the children.

4. The reader will plan a theme on, "Sealife," then allow the children to cut out Sealife and do a mural.

5. You may add your own theme ideals to this list.

_____

_____

_____

_____

_____

_____

SUGGESTED BOOKS

"What Do You Want to Be"
by Lakeshore and Illustrations by Ron Ellsworth

"I Know an Old Lady Who Swallowed A Fly"
by Nadine Bernard Westcott

"Mister Seahorse" by Eric Carle

"The Grochy Ladybug" by Eric Carle

"Pancakes, Pancakes!" by Eric Carle

"Add your own theme books to this list"

_____

_____

_____

_____

_____

_____

VII

ACCELERATED READING

OVERVIEW

An accelerated reading program will give older children, grades third through fifth the practice they need to succeed in their reading and comprehension skills. Students will select a book on their reading level and read that book for 10 to 15 minutes (a timer is set). After the timer goes off, the students are given an oral and a written quiz to test their reading and comprehension skills about the book.

The teacher will keep a log of all test scores that were given throughout the process. This will give the teacher and parent a guide of the progress of the student's reading skills. Accelerated reading is an excellent way to obtain reading performance, and also helps to motivate and monitor students reading progress and vocabulary growth.

SUGGESTED ACTIVITIES

1. The reader will allow the students to read as teams (two students); then give a short oral quiz to see which team scores the highest points.

2. The reader will shorten the reading time to five minutes, then allow students to see how many pages of the book they can finish.

3. The reader will use vocabulary words written on index cards, then allow students to pronounce the words and give definitions.

4. The reader will allow students to earn points by giving the correct answers to an oral quiz about the book. (Students will read the same book).

5. Choose your own accelerated reading ideals.

_____

_____

_____

_____

_____

_____

SUGGESTED BOOKS

"The House That Jack Built" by Rand McNally &Company

"Time to Sleep" by Denise Fleming

"The Giving Tree" by Shel Silverstein

"Bunny Cakes" By Rosemary Wells

"Margaret And Margarita" by Lynn Reiser

_____

_____

_____

_____

_____

_____

VIII

MAKING A BOOK
COME ALIVE

OVERVIEW

The reader can make a book come alive by engaging the children to take part in the story. Encouraging them to participate by asking them questions, allowing them to make silly sounds, allowing them to change their voices, and allowing them to pretend to be characters within the story.

You may throw a little dramatic play in the story by allowing the children to dress-up like the characters within the story. The reader may also use props such as costumes, masks, scarves, hats and banners. The children could fill in parts by adding rhymes, chants, and silly words to spark interest in the story. The reader should not rush through the story, but allow the children to make comments, ask questions, and details about the story being read. This will allow the children to gain an appreciation for reading books, and an excellent learning experience, while having lots of fun.

SUGGESTED ACTIVITIES

1. The reader will allow the children to dress-up in pig masks, while reading the book, "The Three Little Pigs."

2. The reader will read the book, "The Door Bell Rang," then allow the children to make sounds like a door bell.

3. The reader will read the book, "Push, Pull, Empty, Full", then allow the children to act out each word.

4. The reader will allow the children to walk in a sand box barefoot, and afterward read the book, "The Foot Book."

5. You may add your own activities to this list.

_____

_____

_____

_____

_____

SUGGESTED BOOKS

"Push, Pull, Empty, Full" by Tanya Hoban

"The Three Little Pigs" by Troll Associates & Illustration by Eileen Grace

"The Foot Book" by Dr. Seuss

"Where the Wild Things Are" by Maurice Sendak

"The Door Bell Rang" by Pat Hutchins

"Add your own Books to this list"

_____

_____

_____

_____

_____

_____

XI

WORDS, WORDS, WORDS

OVERVIEW

Reading books to children brings words to life. A print rich environment will stimulate children to learn and excel in the reading development. Labeling objects throughout their space with words, words, words, is an excellent way to teach children the meaning of words. This will also give them a rich and wide vocabulary. Introduce older children to vocabulary word list before reading a book. Then allow them to look up the definition of each word. This will help them with reading and comprehension skills. Exposing children to lots of words early in their development will build their language and vocabulary skills.

SUGGESTED ACTIVITIES

1. The reader will introduce a book's word list; then allow children to give the definition of each word.

2. The reader will create a "wall of words chart," then allow the children to circle the words with a marker as the reader reads the book.

3. The reader will use a chart of words; then allow the children to make the same sounds.

4. The reader will use word cards; then allow the children to play a game called, "words around the room."

5. Add your own creative ideals to this list.

_____

_____

_____

_____

_____

_____

SUGGESTED BOOKS

"Five Little Monkeys with Knowing To Do"
by Eileen Christelow

"Henny Penny" by P. Galdone

"Four Fur Feet" by Margaret Wise Brown

"Bones, Bones, Bones Dinosaur Bones" by Byron Barton

"Add your own books to this list."

_____

_____

_____

_____

_____

_____

X

SUPPORTING LANGUAGE AND LITERACY EVERYDAY

OVERVIEW

Language and literacy learning begins at home. Families and caregivers can support children language and literacy explorations by providing an environment filled with books, print, writing tools, songs, pictures, and other interesting things to explore. Families and caregivers can support children by incorporating language and literacy related items in all indoor and outdoor areas used by children. Families and caregivers can support children's use of conversation by asking open-ended questions to expand thinking and understanding during read-aloud sessions and throughout their day.

SUGGESTED ACTIVITIES

1. The reader will introduce the children to games, finger plays, songs, rhymes and chants everyday.

2. The reader will engage children in language and literacy learning.

Example: The reader will provide the children with a variety of materials such as: books, writing materials, puzzles, painting, and will also support their cognitive development by asking open-ended questions.

3. The reader will allow the children to play matching games such as concentration, lotto, or bingo.

4. The reader will allow the children to build with blocks or other materials; then ask them to talk about their projects.

5 "Add your own ideals to this list."

_____

_____

_____

_____

_____

SUGGESTED BOOKS

"Lon Po Po" by Ed Young

"Bread, Bread, Bread" by Ann Morris

"The Random House Book of Poetry for Children"
by Jack Prelutsky

"Right at Home, Family Experiences for Building Literacy"
by Merrily P. Hensen and Gloria Armstrong

"Add your own books to this list"

_____

_____

_____

_____

_____

_____

REFERENCES

Care to Read Manual by Reading Is Fundamental, Inc.

The Creative Curriculum for Early Childhood, Third Edition by Diane Trister Dodge and Laura J. Colker

Read with Me & Read with Me—The Teacher—Parent Partnership by Reading Is Fundamental, Inc.

Hooks, Books, & Cooks by Kim Adsit, & Wendy Gilstrap

Best Practices—on the right track with literacy by The Office of School Readiness Georgia State University

Lakeshore Learning Materials Catalog

Reading Aloud to Young Children—A Guide for Parenting, by Reading Is Fundamental, Inc.